Happy Holiday

Presidents' Day

by Rebecca Sabelko

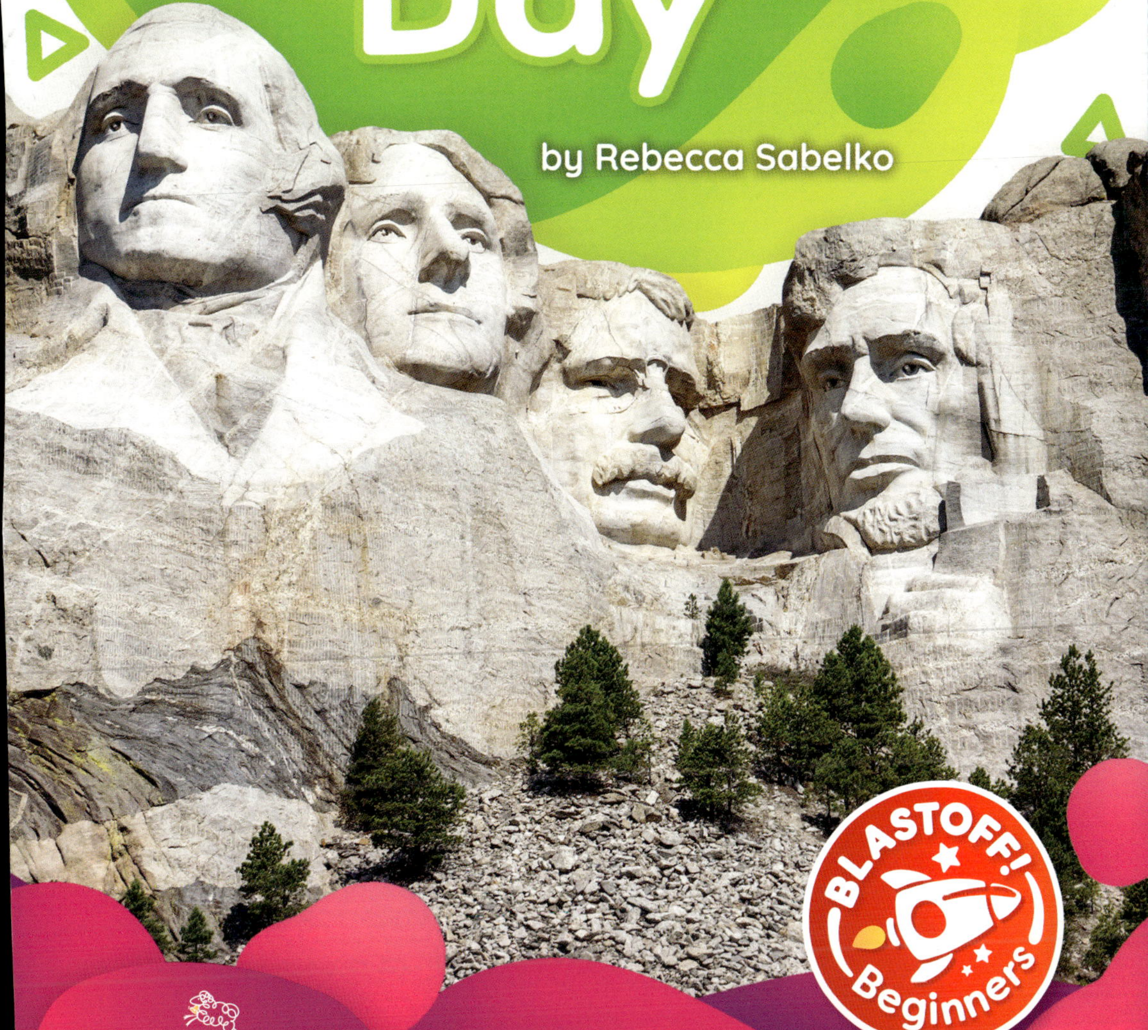

BLASTOFF! Beginners

BELLWETHER MEDIA
MINNEAPOLIS, MN

Blastoff! Beginners are developed by literacy experts and educators to meet the needs of early readers. These engaging informational texts support young children as they begin reading about their world. Through simple language and high frequency words paired with crisp, colorful photos, Blastoff! Beginners launch young readers into the universe of independent reading.

Sight Words in This Book

a	have	many	out	to
about	him	not	people	too
day	in	of	see	we
do	is	other	the	
go	it	our	they	

This edition first published in 2024 by Bellwether Media, Inc.

Library of Congress Cataloging-in-Publication Data

LC record for Presidents' Day available at: https://lccn.loc.gov/2023001667

Editor: Christina Leaf Designer: Laura Sowers

Printed in the United States of America, North Mankato, MN.

Table of Contents

It Is Presidents' Day!

We learn about past leaders. It is Presidents' Day!

What are we learning? (K)
Fish need food, clean water, and space.
Goldfish have 2 eyes, 1 tail, 6 fins, 1 mouth, gills, and scales.
Pennies in a Jar

What Is Presidents' Day?

Presidents’ Day is in February. It is the third Monday.

I HAVE SWORN UPON THE ALTAR OF G

It is near George Washington's birthday.
We honor him!

President George Washington

We honor other presidents, too.

A Day to Honor Leaders

Students learn
about the past.
They have
a day off.

People go to
special places.
They see
the homes
of presidents.

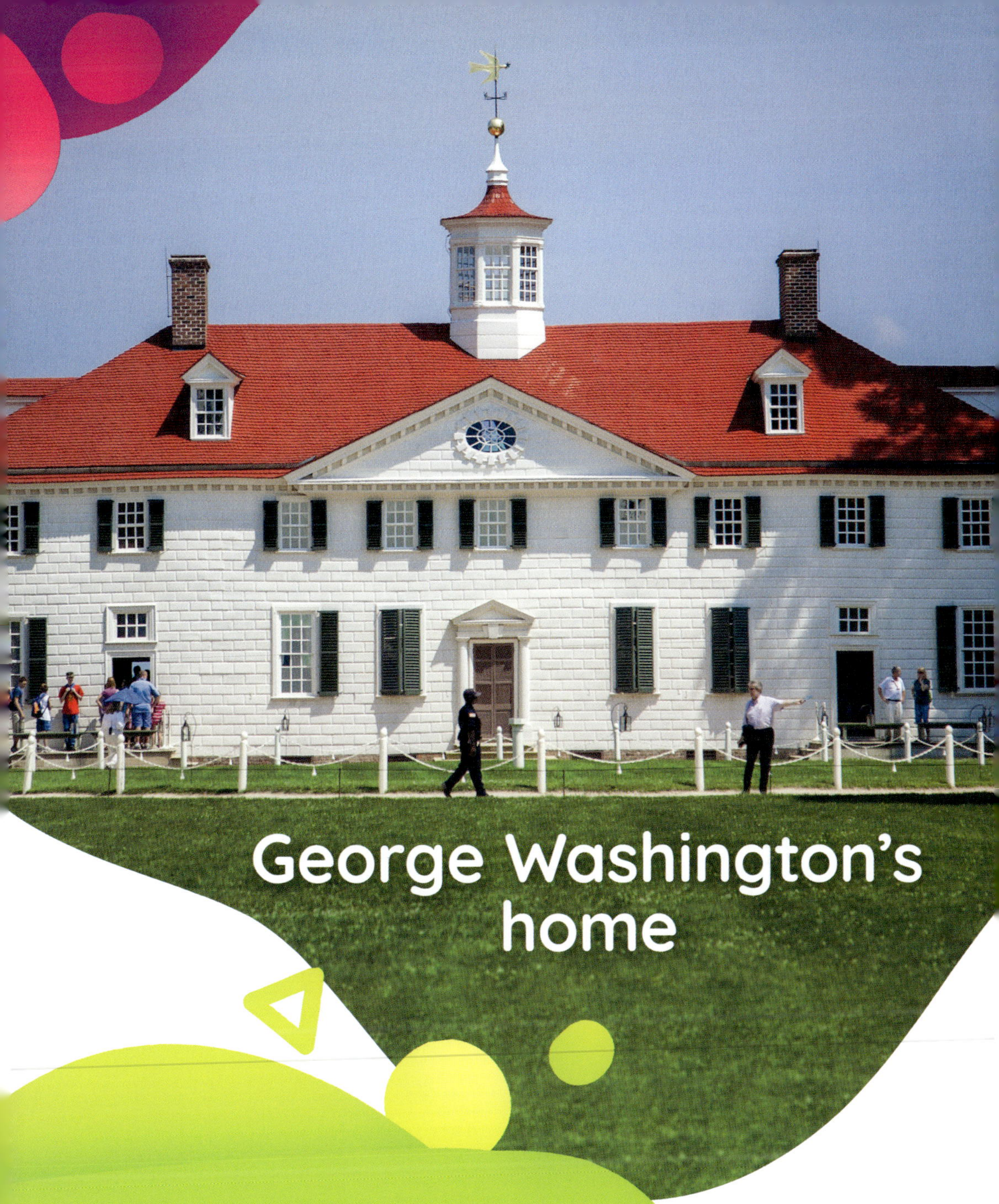

George Washington's home

People act out **history**.
They hear **speeches**.

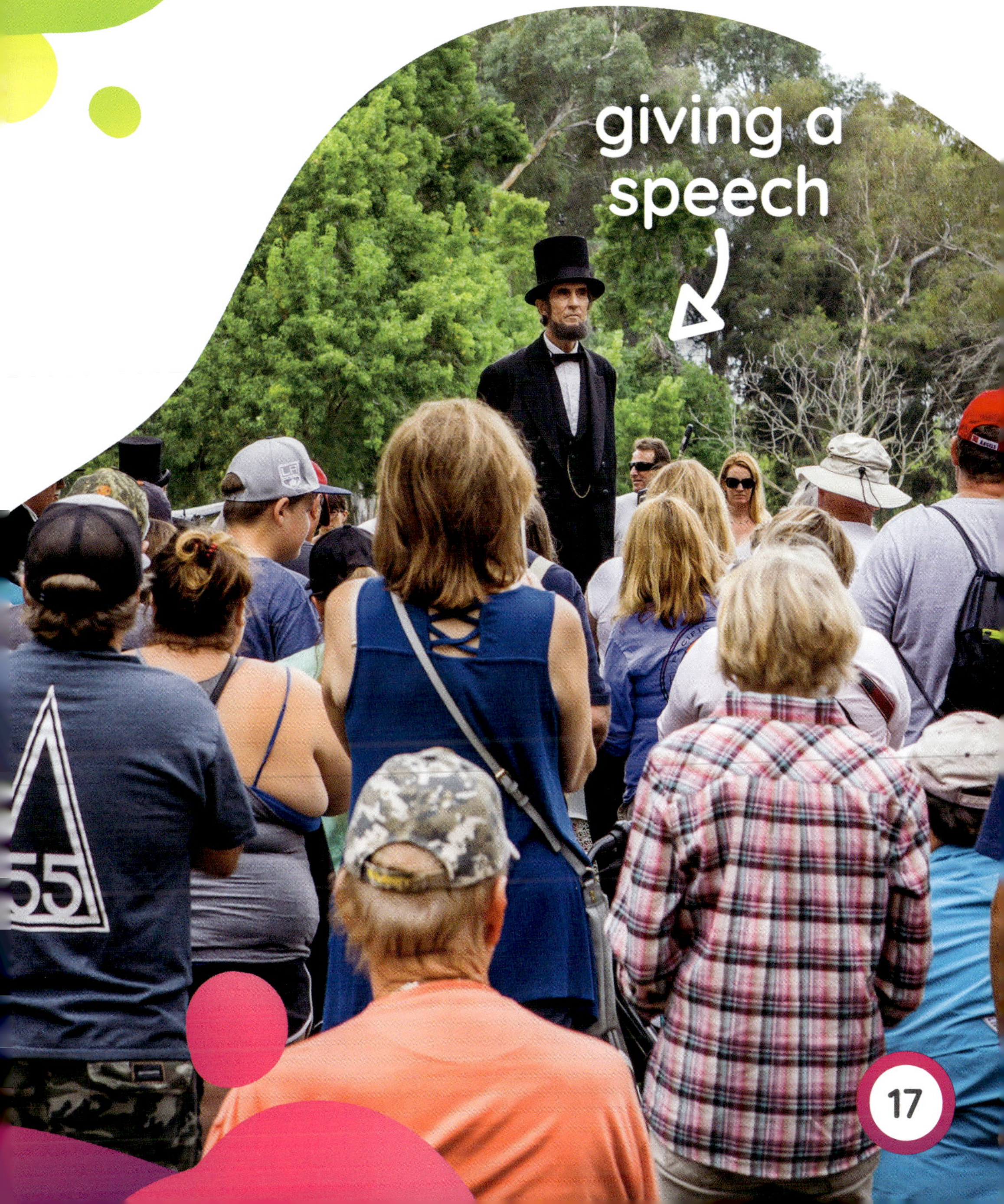
giving a speech

Stores have **sales**. Many people do not have to work.

SALE
UP TO
50%
OFF
SELECTED LINES ONLY
50% off
SALE
50% off

People honor our leaders!

Presidents' Day Facts

Celebrating Presidents' Day

Presidents' Day Activities

learn about the past

see presidents' homes

act out history

Glossary

history

events from the past

sales

events during which goods cost less money

speeches

words spoken for others to hear

To Learn More

ON THE WEB

FACTSURFER

Factsurfer.com gives you a safe, fun way to find more information.

1. Go to www.factsurfer.com.
2. Enter "Presidents' Day" into the search box and click 🔍.
3. Select your book cover to see a list of related content.

Index

The images in this book are reproduced through the courtesy of: Mendenhall Olga, front cover; Peakstock, p. 3; MediaNews Group/ Boston Herald/ Getty Images, pp. 4-5; Rob Crandall/ Alamy, pp. 6-7; Heritage Images/ Getty Images, pp. 8-9; Radharc Images/ Alamy, pp. 10-11; Rawpixel.com, pp. 12-13; Bob Pool, pp. 14-15; Duncan Selby/ Alamy, pp. 16-17; yogoigo, pp. 18-19; Marla Holden/ Alamy, pp. 20-21; James Nesterwitz/ Alamy, p. 22; Jeffrey Isaac Greenberg 7+/ Alamy, p. 22 (learn about the past); Maurice Savage/ Alamy, p. 22 (see presidents' homes); Brian Muck, p. 22 (act out history); Victorian Traditions, p. 23 (history); Tzido Sun, p. 23 (sale); Shirley Preston, p. 23 (speeches).